Bumblebee

Textbook 3

Herausgegeben von
Gisela Ehlers

Erarbeitet von
Gisela Ehlers, Ursula Michailow-Drews,
Anna Van Montagu, Michaela Schönau,
Hannelore Tait, Anne Zeich-Pelsis

Auf der Grundlage von
Bumblebee Textbook 3 (2013/2014) von
Gisela Ehlers, Grit Kahstein, Christina
Meindl, Matthias Muth und Hannelore Tait

Muttersprachliche Beratung
Elspeth Corrie

Illustriert von
Juliane Assies, Jutta Garbert,
Heike Heimrich, Elisabeth Holzhausen,
Oda Ruthe, Friederike Schumann
und Ulrike Vetter

Schroedel
westermann

Contents

▶ Ich kann über viele Themen sprechen.

Welcome

1 Talk about the picture.

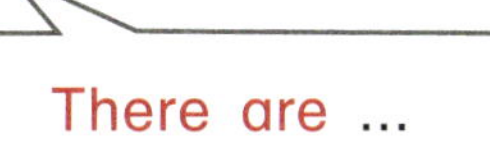

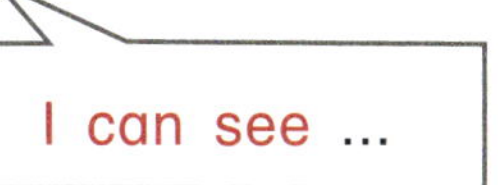

Back to school

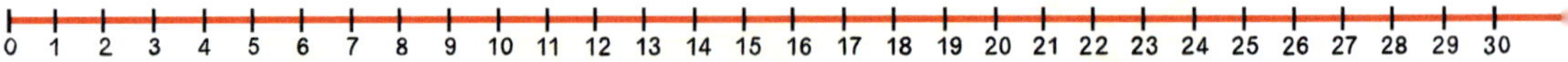

1 Listen and point.

2 Talk about the picture.

3 Do a role-play. Ask questions.

Kennenlerndialoge erweitern/neue Schulsachen lernen.
Diff ▲ KV 8/11, **Diff ▼** KV 7
Wdh: numbers, colours, school things

- FC 1–13, WB S. 4/6
- CD 1/2
- KV 3–11

▶ Ich kann viele Fragen stellen.

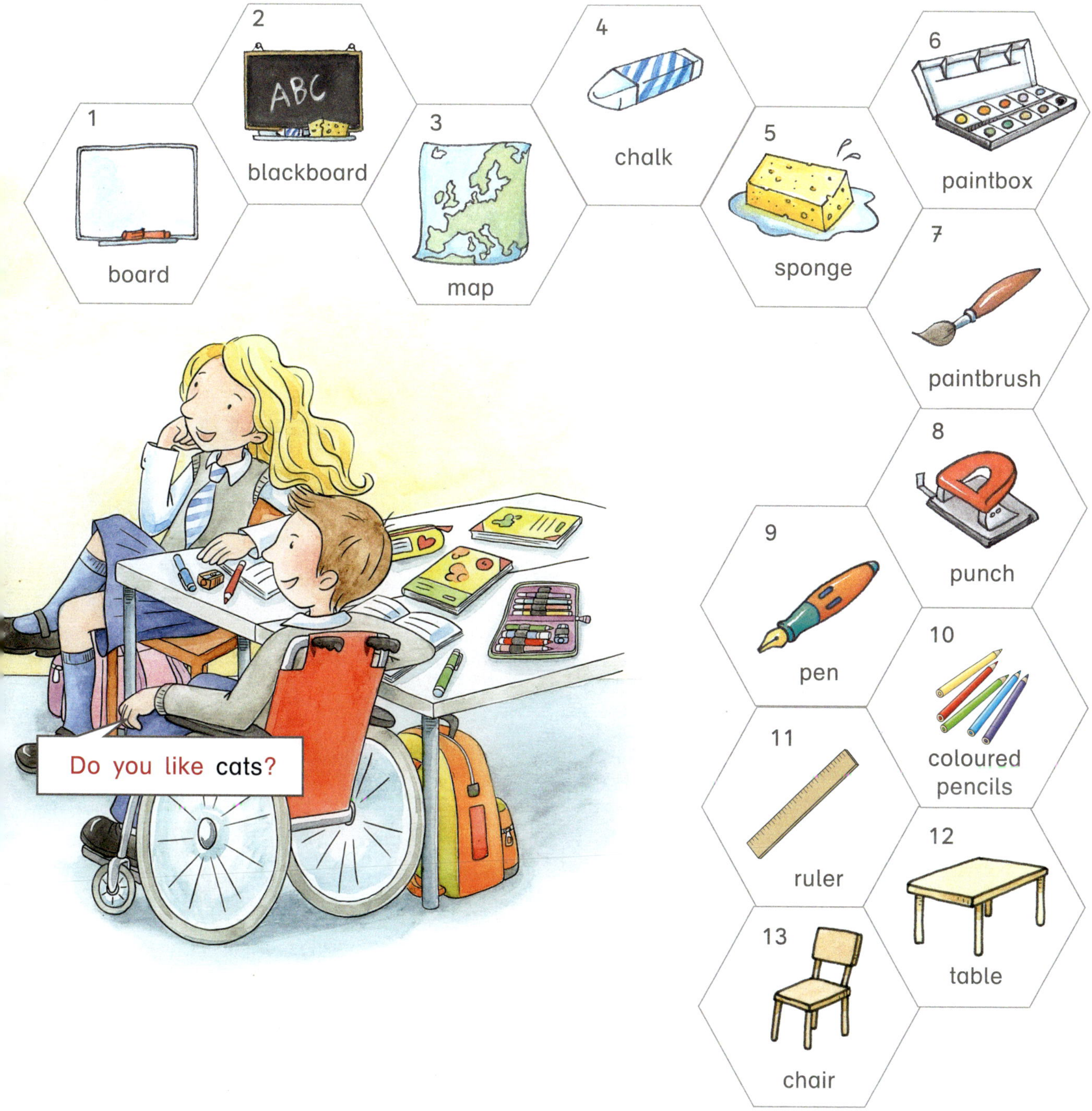

1 board

2 blackboard

3 map

4 chalk

5 sponge

6 paintbox

7 paintbrush

8 punch

9 pen

10 coloured pencils

11 ruler

12 table

13 chair

Where are the children?
How many pencil cases can you see?
What colour is/are ...?

What is the new boy's name?
Where is Jacob from?
What would you like to ask Jacob?

Let's talk: new friends

1 Listen and point.

2 Listen again and read along.

3 Practise the dialogue. 

　Einen Kennenlerndialog führen.

• CD 5
• WB S. 5
• KV 13/14

Jacob from Canada

Hi Leute,

stellt Euch vor, seit heute sind wir ein Kind mehr in meiner Klasse! Jacob ist in den Sommerferien mit seiner Familie aus Kanada nach London gezogen. Wisst Ihr, wo Kanada liegt? Wir haben uns das auf dem Globus angesehen. Ganz schön weit weg.
Mannomann, hatten wir viele Fragen an Jacob. Er hat uns viel von Kanada erzählt. In Kanada spricht man nämlich französisch und englisch. Jacob kommt aus dem Teil, in dem man französisch spricht. Daher muss er auch noch an seinem Englisch arbeiten, wie ich! Jacob hat uns auch viele Fotos mitgebracht. Sein Lieblingssport ist Eishockey. Kennt Ihr das? Ich hab das schon mal im Fernsehen gesehen, aber die Spielregeln muss ich mir noch erklären lassen. So, Schluss für heute. Ich möchte im Internet noch etwas über Kanada herausfinden …

Bis bald,
Lisa

1 Read Lisa's letter. Talk about it.

2 What do you know about Canada? Find information on the internet.

Lisa's new school bus

1

2

3

4

5

6

1 Listen to the story.

2 Listen again and read along.

3 Tell the story in German.

4 Do a role-play.

Eine Geschichte mithilfe von Bildern verstehen.
Diff ▲ KV 16, **Diff ▼** L liest die Geschichte selbst.

• SC 1–6
• CD 7
• KV 16/86

▸ Ich kann einen Rap sprechen.

School rap

2

Hey boys and girls.
Let's go to school.
Let's read and write.
That's great, that's cool.

5

6

Hey boys and girls.
Let's go to school.
Let's count and draw.
That's great, that's cool.

1

4

Hey boys and girls.
Let's go to school.
Let's sing and play.
That's great, that's cool.

3

1 Listen to the rap. 

2 Match the pictures. 

3 Listen and speak along.  

Breakfast with Ben

1 Listen and point.

2 Name five things in the pictures. 

Eine Geschichte mithilfe von Bildern verfolgen.
Diff ▲ KV 22/23, **Diff ▼** L liest die Geschichte selbst.
Wdh: toys

· FC 20–34/SC 7–11
· CD 10/11
· KV 19–23/86

▶ Ich kann Frühstücksgegenstände benennen.

Who is in bed?
Who wakes Ben up?
What is the name of the dog?

What is in Ben's muesli?
What is on the breakfast table?
What is on your breakfast table?

► Ich kann sagen, was ich in meiner Brotdose haben möchte.

Let's talk: What would you like in your lunchbox?

1 Listen and read along.  

2 What would you like in your lunchbox? 

Höflich um etwas bitten und es überreichen.
Diff ▲ ▼ KV 24
Wdh: food

· CC 3–9, WB S. 9
· CD 14
· KV 24

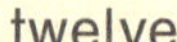

▶ Ich kann ein englisches Frühstück beschreiben.

An English breakfast

Hallo Ihr in Deutschland,

es ist Samstag und ich habe gerade ein tolles englisches Frühstück gegessen. Es schmeckte super! Aber es war ganz schön viel. Ein englisches Frühstück läuft so ab: Zuerst gibt es Saft, dann Müsli oder Cornflakes. Danach isst man Eier mit Speck, Würstchen und Bohnen in Tomatensoße (*bacon and eggs, sausages and baked beans*). Wer dann noch Hunger hat, kann auch noch Toast mit Butter und Marmelade frühstücken. Dazu trinkt man Tee, Kaffee oder Kakao. Meine Eltern sagen, wenn wir das jeden Tag essen würden, wären wir bald kugelrund. Das ist vielleicht der Grund, warum die Briten dieses Frühstück nur am Wochenende essen und unter der Woche Müsli oder Toast. Hier kennen aber auch alle Nussnougatcreme (*chocolate nut spread*) und viele Kinder nehmen ein Sandwich mit Nussnougatcreme in ihrer Brotdose (*lunchbox*) mit zur Schule.

Eure sehr satte

Lisa

1 Read Lisa's letter. 

2 Compare English breakfast with German breakfast.

How to make a sandwich

This is what you need:

Put salami and cheese on top.

Put bread on top. Cut it in half.

Butter the bread.

Add cucumber.

Put your sandwich in your lunchbox.

1 Look at the pictures. 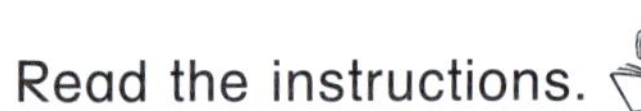

2 Read the instructions.

3 Talk about your favourite sandwich. 

4 Make your own sandwich.

Eine bildgestützte Anleitung verstehen.
Diff ▼ L spielt die Anleitung von CD Track 15 vor oder liest sie selbst.

· How to read S. 54
· CD 15

▸ Ich kann lustige Fragen stellen und beantworten.

Breakfast game

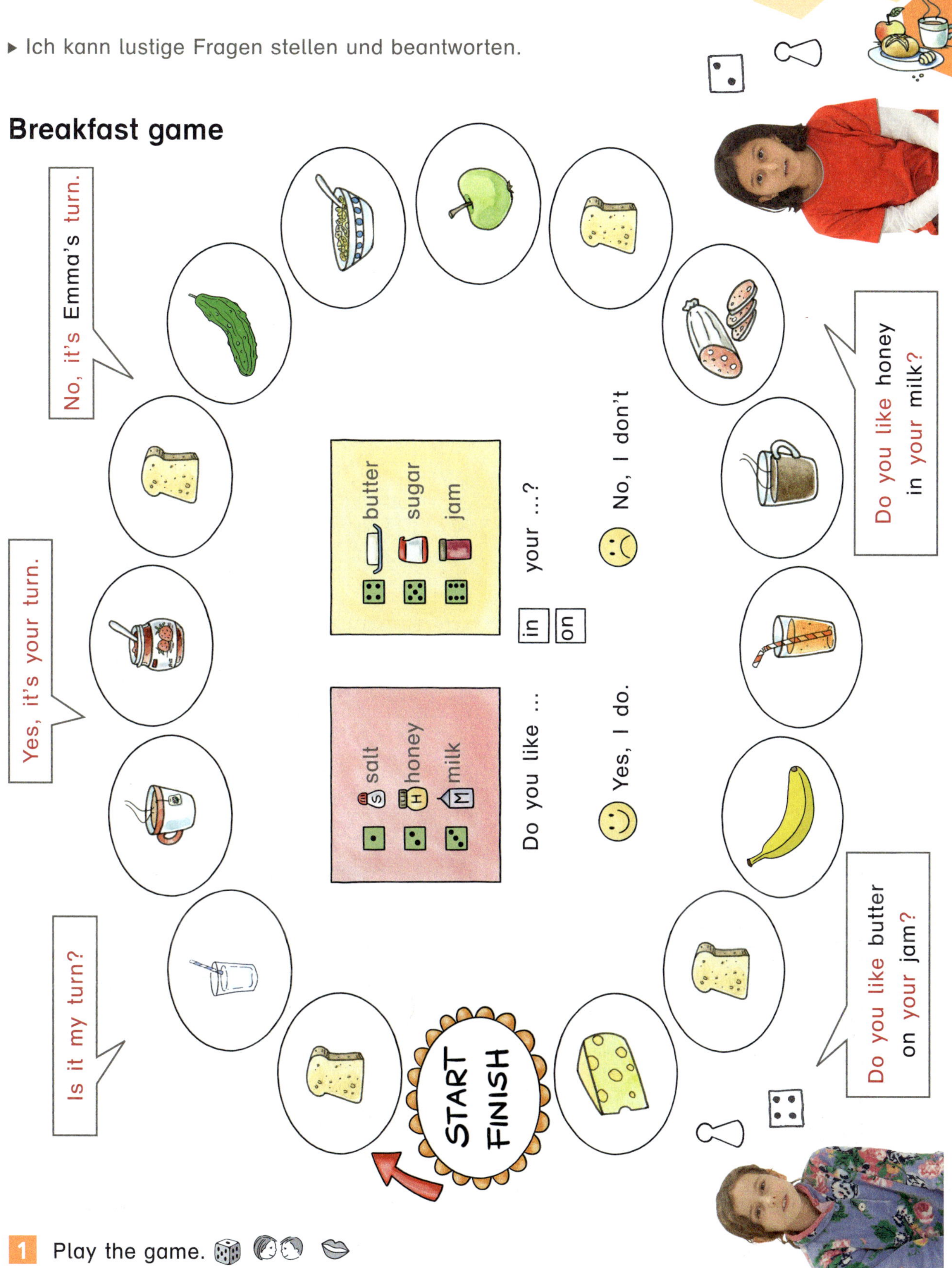

1 Play the game.

Shopping

1 Listen and point.

2 Read the dialogues and the menu.

3 Make up your own dialogue.

Wörter und Redemittel zum Thema „Einkaufen" kennenlernen.
Diff ▲ KV 30–32, Spiel: *I spy*, **Diff** ▼ KV 30
Wdh: toys, fruit, vegetables, numbers

• FC 35–52, WB S. 56
• CD 17/18
• KV 28–32/91

4 What is your favourite shop?

5 Make a shopping centre poster. Use a dictionary.

What can you name in the picture?
How many people can you see?
What would you like to buy?

What is the boy eating?
What would you like to eat and drink?

Let's talk: buying an ice cream

1 Listen and point. 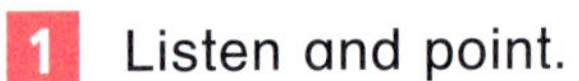

2 Listen and read along.  

3 Practise the dialogue. 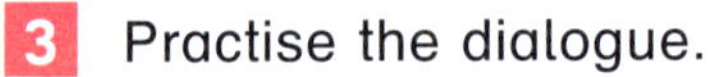

4 Write about your favourite ice cream.  

Einen Einkaufsdialog führen.
Diff ▼ KV 33, **Diff ▲** individuelle Dialoge vorspielen
Wdh: What's your favourite ...?, fruit

- CC 13–17, WB S. 14
- CD 19
- KV 33

English money

Hallo Ihr,

obwohl Großbritannien zu Europa gehört, wird hier nicht mit dem Euro bezahlt, sondern mit Pfund (*pounds*) und *pence*. Das Zeichen £ steht für *pound* und *p* für *pence*. Einen einzigen *pence* nennt man übrigens auch *penny*. Auf vielen Geldscheinen ist die Queen abgebildet. Die Abbildungen von ihr auf den Geldscheinen werden immer wieder angepasst, sodass die Queen auch auf den Geldscheinen älter wird. Lustig, oder? Mein Sparschwein hat hier übrigens auch einen sehr schönen Namen: die *piggy bank*. Ich habe Euch noch ein paar Fotos von meinen Lieblingsläden mitgeschickt. Schön, oder?

Liebe Grüße und bis bald,

Lisa

1 Read Lisa's letter. Compare German and British money.  

The headphones

Eine Geschichte mithilfe von Bildern verstehen.
Diff ▲ KV 35, Texte für Kims Gedankenblasen erfinden.

• SC 12–19
• CD 21
• KV 35/86

1. Listen to the story. What is it about?

2. Listen again and point.

3. Act it out.

4. Read Kim's list. Write your own list: I can …

My busy week

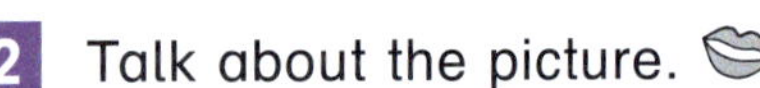

1 Listen and point.

2 Talk about the picture.

3 Name 2 of your daily routines.

4 Make a poster and present it. 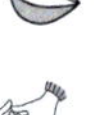

Über Tagesabläufe sprechen lernen.
Diff ▲ KV 40/44, **Diff ▼** KV 43
Wdh: hobbies, activities

- FC/WC 55–84
- CD 23/24
- KV 37–44

He, she, it –
das s muss mit!

MONDAY
TUESDAY
WEDNESDAY
THURSDAY
FRIDAY
SATURDAY
SUNDAY

18
watch TV

17
meet
my friends

16
feed
my pet

15
go cycling

14
play
hockey

13
go
skateboarding

12
play the
recorder

11
collect
football
stickers

10
evening

9
afternoon

8
morning

7
7
Sun
Sunday

1
1
Mon
Monday

2
2
Tue
Tuesday

3
3
Wed
Wednesday

4
4
Thu
Thursday

5
5
Fri
Friday

6
6
Sat
Saturday

Days of the week

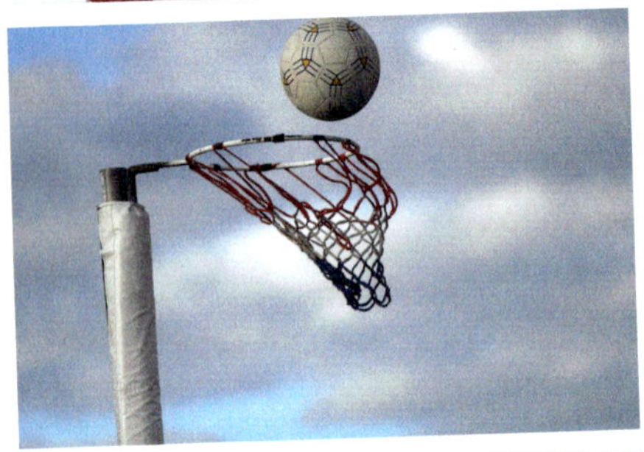

Hallo Ihr,

hier an meiner Schule gibt es viele *school clubs*. Es gibt *school clubs* für verschiedene Sportarten, für Theater oder auch Handarbeiten. Ich habe mich für eine hier sehr beliebte Sportart entschieden, sie heißt *netball*. *Netball* wird meistens nur von Mädchen gespielt und geht ganz ähnlich wie Basketball. Eine Mannschaft besteht aus sieben Spielerinnen. Es wird 4 mal 15 Minuten gespielt. Zwei Regeln finde ich gut: Es gibt keinen Körperkontakt, also auch kein Anrempeln. Außerdem wird nicht gedribbelt. Dribbeln konnte ich nämlich noch nie gut. Wenn Ihr mehr darüber wissen möchtet, schaut doch mal im Internet nach.

Eure netballbegeisterte Lisa

1 Read Lisa's letter. Talk about it.   

2 Sing the Weekend song. 

Landeskundliche Informationen erhalten.
Ein Lied zu den Wochentagen lernen.

• CD 25/26
• KV 45

Emma's diary

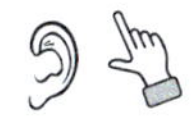

DAYS	Emma	Dad	Tim	Mum
Monday	cycling with Janet			
Tuesday	school outing to the zoo	tennis		
Wednesday	meet Ben and Ravi			
Thursday				
Friday	football			
Saturday	swimming with Dad ♥			
Sunday				

1 Listen and point to the days. 

2 Listen again. When will Emma, Ben and Ravi meet?

3 Talk about your week.

4 Find activities for Tim and Mum. 

Lots of hobbies

1 Read the hobbies.

2 Talk about the children's hobbies. 

   Über Hobbys und Vorlieben sprechen.

• CC 19/20
• KV 47

▸ Ich kann mich mit anderen zum Spielen verabreden.

Let's talk: When can we meet to play?

1 Ask a question.

2 Spin the bottle.

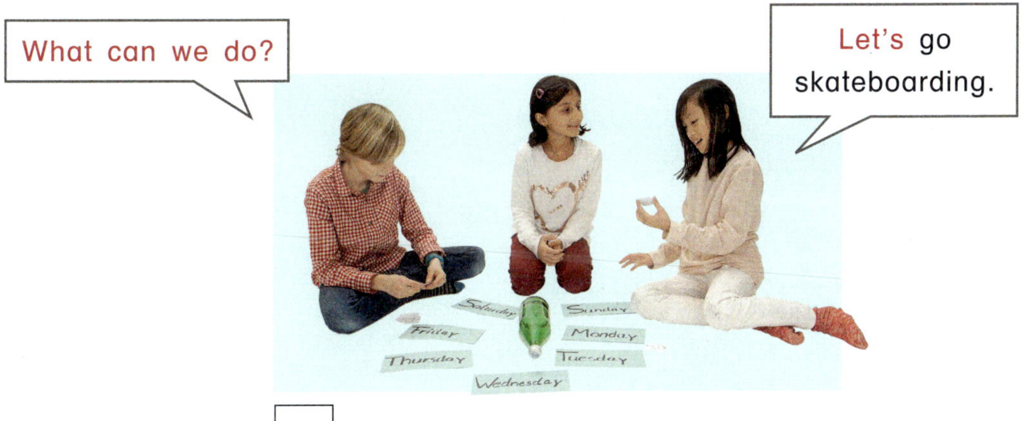

3 Take a Bingo card. Say the sentence.

1 Listen to the dialogue.

2 Practise the dialogue. 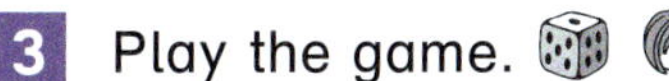

3 Play the game.  

Dress for the weather

1 Listen and point.

2 Talk about the picture.

Kleidungsstücke, Wetter und Jahreszeiten benennen.
Diff ▲ KV 51, **Diff** ▼ KV 52/53
Wdh: colours

- FC/WC 85–114
- CD 30/31
- KV 48–53

▶ Ich kann Wetterlagen und Kleidungsstücke benennen.

What are the children doing?
How many gloves /... can you see?
What can you see/read on the board?

Can you name the seasons?
What is your favourite season?

I like blue jeans

Text/Musik: V. Binder/B. Walla/F. Moser

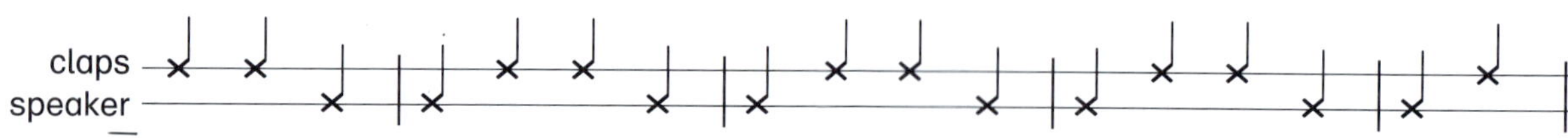

2. I like green socks … and pink shirts.
3. I like pink shirts … and black caps.
4. I like black caps … and red shoes.
5. I like red shoes … and blue jeans.

Hallo Ihr in Deutschland,

gestern hatten wir in der Schule Besuch von *Brownies* und *Cubs* – nein, das ist nichts zum Essen! Uns haben Pfadfinder besucht. Die Mädchen nennen sich Brownies und die Jungen Cubs. Toll fand ich ihre Kleidung. Die Mädchen tragen eine blaue Bluse mit passendem Halstuch und braunem Rock. Die Jungen eine braune Hose, ein blaues Hemd und ein blaues Cap. Das sieht schick aus. Besonders gefallen hat mir, was sie über ihre Aktivitäten erzählt haben: Gemeinsames Basteln, Erste-Hilfe-Kurse, Ausflüge und gemeinsames Spielen. Und ihre Ausflüge! Da wird in Zelten geschlafen und gemeinsam gekocht. Ich werde demnächst mitmachen, denn wir wurden zu einem gemeinsamen Camping-Wochenende eingeladen. Die Brownies und Cubs gibt es nicht nur in Großbritannien, sondern auch in den USA und in Kanada. Einige pflegen sogar Brieffreundschaften miteinander. Im Internet findet man jede Menge über sie … Ich freue mich schon auf mein Gastwochenende bei den Brownies.
Bis bald,

Eure Lisa

1 Listen and sing the song. 

2 Read Lisa's letter. Compare to Germany. 

Landeskundliche Informationen über Pfadfinder
in englischsprachigen Ländern erhalten.

• CD 32/33

▸ Ich kann sagen, welche Kleidung ich einpacken muss.

Let's talk: Weather forecast

1 Listen to the dialogue.

2 Practise the dialogue.

3 Find a weather forecast. Pack for a weekend. 

Weather massage

 Many little raindrops are falling on the ground.
Oh what's that? The sky is grey.
I can see the clouds. 

 Many little raindrops are falling on the ground.
Oh what's that? The wind blows.
I can feel the breeze. 

 Many little raindrops are falling on the ground.
Oh what's that? There is a flash.
I can see the lightning. 

 Many little raindrops are falling on the ground.
Oh what's that? There is a rumble.
I can hear the thunder. 

 Many little raindrops are falling on the ground.
Oh what's that? The sun comes out.
I can see a rainbow. 

1 Listen and point. 

2 Do the weather massage.  

3 Play a guessing game. Mime the weather.

Die Wettererscheinungen festigen.
Diff ▼ KV 58

• CD 36
• KV 58

▶ Ich kann sagen, was wir in welcher Jahreszeit machen können.

What can we do in ...?

1 
2 
3 
4 
5 
6 
7 
8

1 Listen and point to the pictures.

2 Listen to the dialogue.

3 Make a poster. Label it.

Sugarbush farm

1 Listen and point.

2 Roll 2 dice and name the word.

3 What can you buy at the farm shop?

Wörter und Redemittel zum Thema „Farm" kennenlernen.
Diff ▲ KV 64, Diff ▲ ▼ KV 69
Wdh: pets, colours, numbers

• FC/WC 115–129
• CD 39/40
• KV 62–65/69

▶ Ich kann sagen, was es auf einem Bauernhof gibt.

What can you name in the picture?
How many cats/dogs/cows ... can you see?
What can you buy at the farm shop?

What would you like to buy at the farm shop?
What are your favourite farm animals?
Four horses: How many legs?

Let's talk: What you can do on Sugarbush farm

1 Listen and read along. 

3 Make your own dialogue.  

2 Practise the dialogue. 

Über Aktivitäten auf einem Bauernhof sprechen.
Diff ▼ KV 68
Wdh: What would you like …?

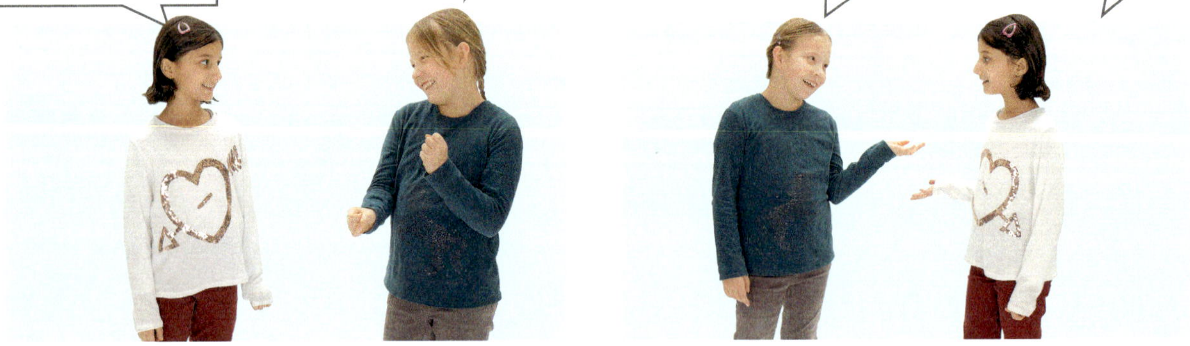

• WB S. 25
• CD 41
• KV 68

► Ich kann etwas über Border Collies erzählen.

Border Collies

Hallo Ihr in Deutschland,

am Wochenende sind wir raus aus der Stadt aufs Land gefahren.
Papa hatte die Nase voll von den Staus in London und freute sich auf leere
Straßen. Aber schon nach ein paar Kilometern steckten wir wieder im Stau.
Keine Angst, es war kein Unfall; eine riesige Schafherde stand mitten auf
der Straße! Die Schäferin stand in der Nähe, gab ein Handzeichen und pfiff.
Ein toller Hund rannte hin und her und versuchte, die Schafe schnell über
die Straße zu treiben. Der Hund war ein Border Collie, einer der
beliebtesten Hütehunde. Border Collies wurden in England gezüchtet, im
Grenzland zwischen England und Schottland. Grenze heißt auf Englisch
border, daher stammt ihr Name. Ich hätte sehr gerne einen Border Collie,
aber Mama sagt, das sind Arbeitshunde, die sich in der Stadt schrecklich
langweilen würden. So ein Pech!
Eure hundelose Lisa

1 Read Lisa's letter.

2 Compare to Germany. Are there similar dogs?

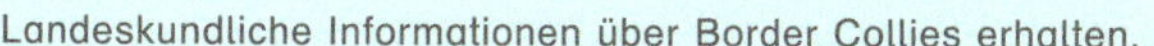

Guess the animal

leg

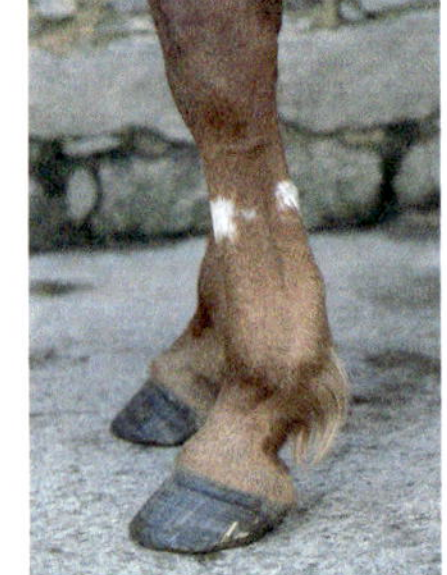

beak

tail

wing

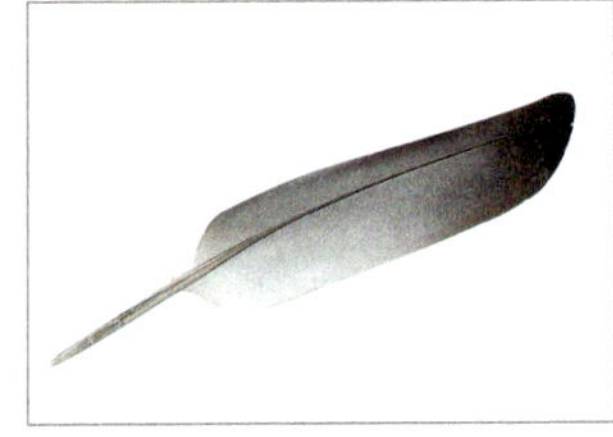

feather

fur

1 Listen and guess.  

2 Write your own animal riddle.

3 Ask questions. Guess your partner's animal.

Tierrätsel stellen und erraten können.
Diff ▲ ▼ KV 67/70
Wdh: colours, numbers, body parts

• CD 42
• KV 67/70

There was an old lady who swallowed a fly

 old lady  fly

There was an  who swallowed a  .

I don't know why she swallowed a  – perhaps she'll die.

There was an  who swallowed a 

that wriggled and wiggled and tiggled inside her.

She swallowed the  to catch the  .

I don't know why she swallowed a  – perhaps she'll die.

1

2

3

4

 **1** Listen and point. 

 **2** Sing along.

A trip to London

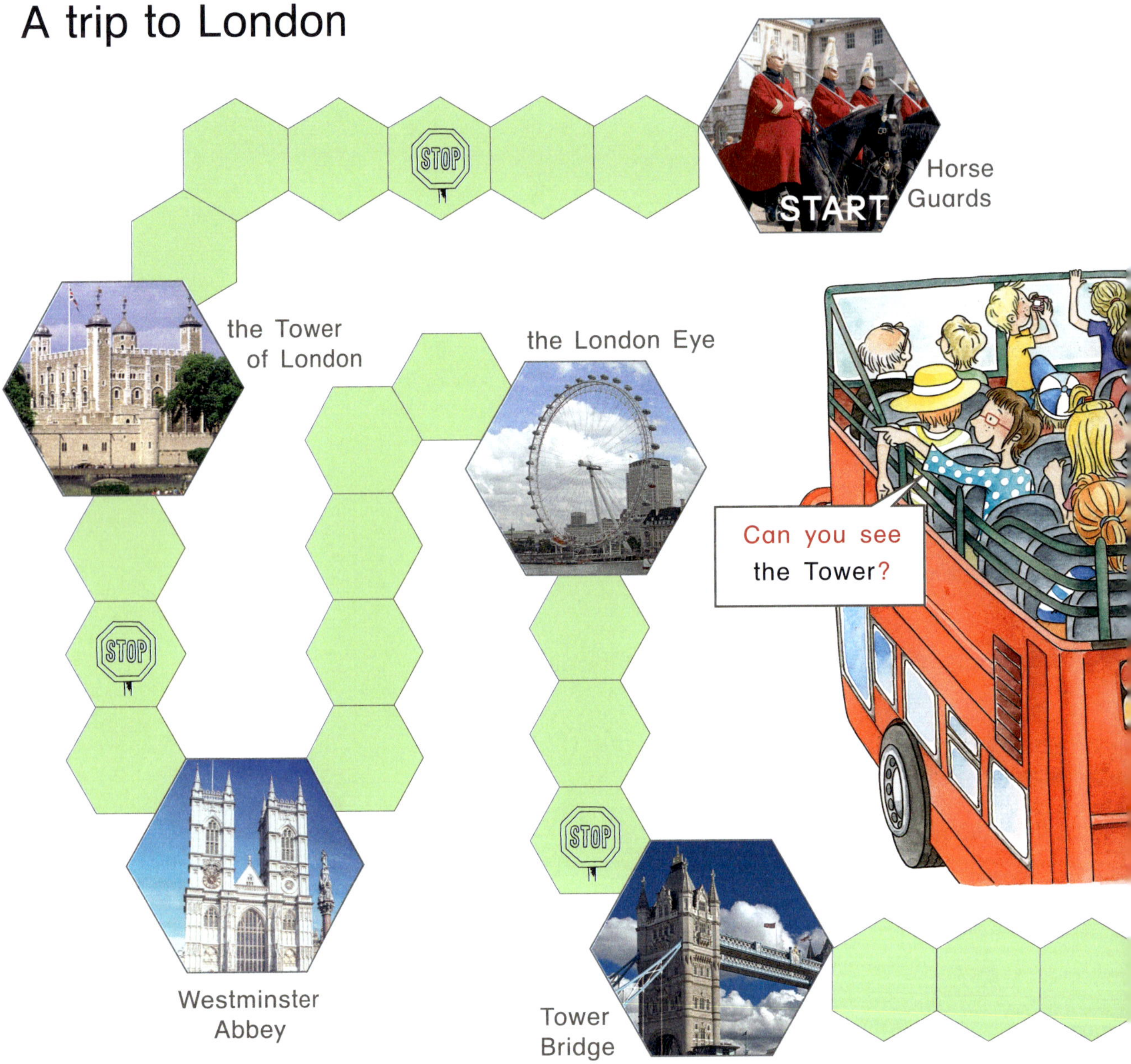

START — Horse Guards

the Tower of London

the London Eye

Westminster Abbey

Tower Bridge

1 Listen and point to the pictures.

2 Listen to the sounds of London.

3 Play the game. 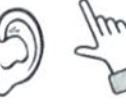

4 Find more information about London sights.

Roll the dice.
Move your counter.
 Miss a turn.

Sehenswürdigkeiten von London kennenlernen.
Diff ▲ KV 75/80, **Diff** ▼ KV 74
Wdh: What would you like to see …?

• Finding information S. 57
• FC 130–148, CD 48–50
• KV 72–75/80

▶ Ich kann ein Spiel zu Londoner Sehenswürdigkeiten spielen.

Buckingham
Palace

FINISH

Big Ben

Hyde Park

London
Zoo

1 ferris wheel

2 palace

3 church

4 bridge

5 taxi

6 double-decker bus

8 turn right

7 underground

10 go straight ahead

9 turn left

What are the children doing?
How many people are on the bus?
How can you get around in London?

What would you like to see in London?
Which sights do you have in your home town?

A day in Hyde Park

Hi Leute,

heute war schönes Wetter und wir haben wie viele Londoner den

Sonntag im Hyde Park verbracht. Erst haben wir wie immer Fußball gespielt,

dann waren wir im *Diana Memorial Fountain* planschen. Das ist eine Art Brunnen, in

dem man waten kann. Nach einem tollen Picknick wollte Martin noch zum großen See,

the Serpentine, und ein Tretboot mieten. Das war super!

Weil wir so müde waren, sind wir dann mit der U-Bahn, der *tube*, heimgefahren.

Die Londoner U-Bahn ist übrigens die älteste U-Bahn der Welt.

Sie wurde 1863 eröffnet. Auf den Rolltreppen, den *escalators*, die zu den

U-Bahnen hinunterführen, sollte man eine wichtige Regel beachten:

Stand on the right. Denn nur so können Fahrgäste, die es eilig haben,

gut an den anderen vorbei kommen. Wer sich nicht an diese Regel hält,

macht sich bei den Londonern sehr unbeliebt. Und auch ganz wichtig:

Mind the gap. Habt Ihr eine Idee, was das bedeuten könnte?

Ratet doch mal! Das Foto hier rechts hilft euch dabei.

Eure müde

Lisa

1 Read Lisa's letter. Talk about it.   

2 Find more information on London.

Landeskundliche Informationen über den Hyde Park und
die Londoner U-Bahn erhalten.

• Finding information S. 57
• KV 78

▶ Ich kann in einem Café etwas bestellen.

Let's talk: at Hyde Park Café

snacks
scone w/ butter and jam
apple crumble
lemon cake
ice cream
fruit salad

food
fish and chips
chicken sandwich
salad
curry
carrot soup

drinks
coffee
tea
hot chocolate
lemonade
juice

1 Listen and practise the dialogue. 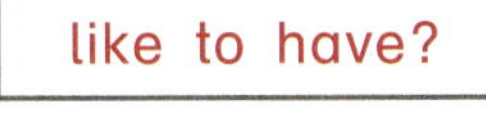

2 Read the menu. What would you like to have? 

3 Write: I'd like to have ... 

A tour in the London Eye

Buckingham Palace is a huge palace.
The Royal Family lives there.

Big Ben ist the biggest bell
in the clock tower of the
Palace of Westminster.

Tower Bridge is a huge
bridge over the River Thames.

The River Thames is the
longest river in England.

1 Listen and point. 

2 Read along.

3 Write about a sight. 

Kurzen Lesetexten Informationen entnehmen.
Diff ▲ KV 77/79

• FC/WC 134–136/139
• CD 54
• KV 77/79

Information: The London Eye

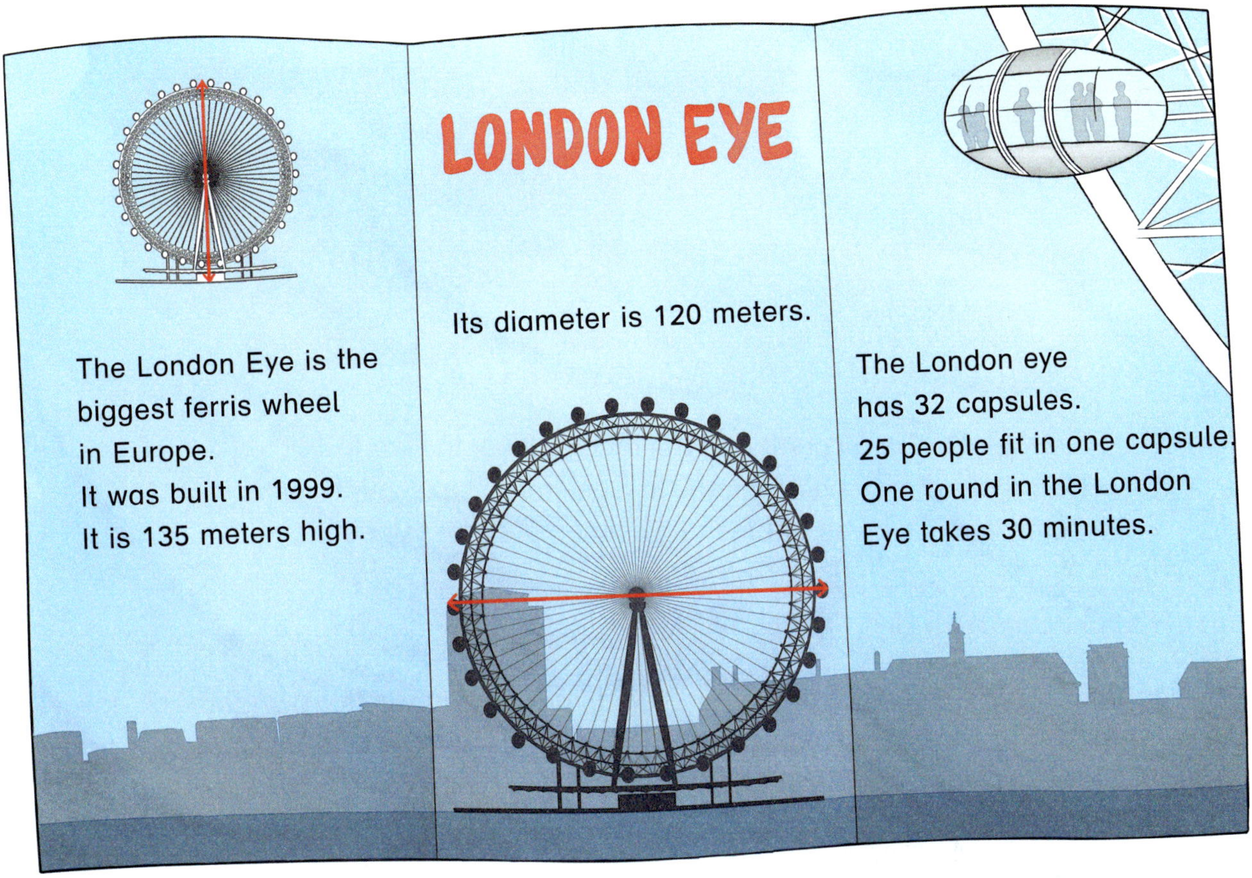

1 Read the text. 

2 Talk in German about the London Eye.

3 How many people can be in the London Eye? 

Christmas around the world

New Zealand is a country on the other side of the world.
It consists of two main islands. In December it is summer there.
Some families celebrate their Christmas party at the beach.

In Great Britain and the USA families have a big Christmas dinner. Sometimes they put on crowns and pull Christmas crackers.
The children hang up stockings on the 24th of December.
They get their presents on the morning of the 25th of December.

1 Listen and point to the pictures. 

2 Talk about the pictures. 

3 How do you celebrate Christmas? Talk. 

Unterschiedliche Weihnachtsbräuche kennenlernen.
Diff ▲ Weihnachtsprojekt: Poster zu Weihnachtsfesten in unterschiedlichen Kulturen erstellen.

• CD 56
• KV 84

In Japan Christmas is popular, too.
People meet with friends and they bake a big strawberry birthday cake for Baby Jesus.

In Spain people celebrate Christmas on the 6th of January.
They buy each other presents and eat a special cake,
the Rosco the Reyes. In this cake there is a little figure.
Whoever gets the piece with the figure is king of the day.

4 Find out more about Christmas in different countries.

Through the year

People send nice cards,
poems or flowers to their friends.

People look for chocolate eggs
and bunnies in the garden.

January	February	March	April	May	June
July	August	September	October	November	December

Children dress up as witches or
ghosts and go from house to house.

People welcome the New Year
with colourful fireworks.

1 Listen and point to the months.

2 Read the texts. When are the special days? Talk.

3 Which special day is missing?

Feste und Monate benennen können.
Diff ▼ KV 83
Wdh: festivals

• FC/WC 149–160
• CD 58
• KV 81–83

Pancake Day

Hallo Ihr Lieben,

schade, dass es hier in Großbritannien keinen Fasching gibt! Aber wenn Ihr in Deutschland am Faschingsdienstag verkleidet zur Schule geht, feiern wir den *Pancake Day*. Früher wurden hier nämlich am Faschingsdienstag noch schnell alle Eier und die Butter aufgebraucht und Pfannkuchen gebacken, da am Aschermittwoch die Fastenzeit beginnt. Es gibt hier eine lustige Tradition, das Pfannkuchenrennen. Nach einer Legende hat eine Frau im Jahr 1445 vor lauter Pfannkuchenbacken vergessen, dass sie in die Kirche musste. Sie ist mit der Pfanne in der Hand losgerannt und hat den Pfannkuchen immer in die Luft geworfen, damit er nicht anbrennt.

Auch heute werden noch solche Rennen veranstaltet. Wer mitmachen will, muss eine Schürze und einen Schal tragen und die Pfannkuchen an der Start- und an der Zielline in die Luft werfen und wieder fangen. Das ist sehr lustig! Bei uns an der Schule gibt es auch ein Pfannkuchenrennen. Wir laufen für einen guten Zweck und essen wahnsinnig viele Pfannkuchen.

Eure kugelrunde Lisa

1 Read Lisa's letter. Talk about it.

Jack and the beanstalk

 money    market    magic beans    cow

 giant    hen    golden eggs    axe

 man    castle    beanstalk

There is a boy named Jack.

He lives with his mother. They have no  **.**

One day Jack's mother says, "**We must sell our**  . Take it to the  ."

On his way to the  Jack meets a  .

The  **gives Jack 5** 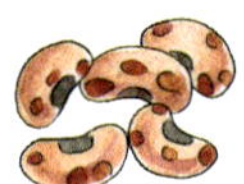 **for the**  **.**

Jack's mother is very angry.

She throws the 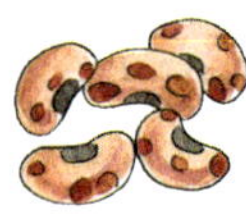 **out of the window.**

  1 Listen to the story. What is it about?   3 Tell the story in German.

2 Read the text out loud.   4 Act it out.

Eine bildgestützte Geschichte verstehen.
Diff ▼ L liest die Geschichte selbst.   • CD 59

The next morning, **there is a big**  in front of the window.

Jack climbs up the . He climbs up higher and higher.

When he is at the top, **Jack sees a beautiful** . **He goes inside.**

There is a big  sleeping in the kitchen.

The  **has a**  **that can lay**  .

Jack takes the  **to take it home.**

Suddenly the  wakes up and runs after Jack.

Jack runs faster. He climbs down the  .

The  **runs after him.**

Jack shouts, "Mother, help, help!"

Jack's mother takes an  **and cuts down the**  .

The  falls to the ground.

Nobody ever sees the  **again.** And Jack and his mother?

They live happily ever after and the  **lays many**  .

How to understand and learn words

Ich achte auf die Bewegungen und das Gesicht meiner Lehrkraft.

Ich höre mir das Wort auf der CD an und spreche es nach.

Ich suche nach einer Eselsbrücke.

Das hilft mir beim Verstehen und Wörterlernen.

Ich schaue mir die Bilder zum Text an.

Ich sage mir das Wort immer wieder laut vor.

Ich versuche, Ähnlichkeiten zum Deutschen zu nutzen.

Ich bewege mich beim Aufsagen der Wörter.

Ich spiele mit meinen Kärtchen ein Wörterspiel wie Find the pairs oder Dominoes.

How to speak

Bei neuen Wörtern höre ich
meiner Lehrkraft genau zu
und spreche ihr dann nach.

Ich höre mir
die CD an
und spreche die
Wörter nach.

Ich versuche, in Sätzen zu
sprechen (die roten Wörter
helfen mir dabei).

Ich frage meine Lehrkraft,
wenn mir ein Wort fehlt.

Ich benutze Gesicht,
Arme und Hände.

Wenn mir ein Wort nicht einfällt,
versuche ich es zu umschreiben
oder zeige darauf, wenn es in
meiner Nähe ist.

Ich höre mir
den Lesetext an.

Ich schlage
unbekannte Wörter
nach.

**Das hilft
mir beim
Lesen.**

Ich suche nach
bekannten Wörtern.

Ich achte auf
helfende Bilder.

Auch wenn ich nicht alle
Wörter verstehe,
kann ich mir den Inhalt
des Textes vorstellen.

Ich achte auf
die Überschrift.

How to copy words correctly

Ich schaue mir das Wort an,
decke es ab, schreibe es
auswendig auf und kontrolliere
mein Geschriebenes.

Ich markiere
Aufpassstellen im Wort.

Das hilft mir beim Abschreiben von Wörtern.

Ich sage mir die Wörter
im Kopf so vor, wie ich
sie in meiner Muttersprache
aussprechen würde.

Ich schreibe das Wort ab und
kontrolliere mein Geschriebenes.

Ich denke mir
Eselsbrücken aus.

Think, pair, share: our shopping centre poster

1 Think
Write down what you would like to buy
at the shopping centre.

2 Pair
Find a partner.
Talk.

3 Share
Find 2 more partners.
Collect all your ideas.
Create a poster.

4 Presentation
Present your poster to the class.

 Make a poster.

Finding information: Canada/London

Go to a library. Look for books or DVDs.

Find information online. Your teacher can help you.

Write to tourist infos and ask for brochures.

Look at newspapers or magazines.

Look for tourist guide books for children.

Look at your English book on pages 40–45.

Go to a travel agency. Ask for brochures.

Ask people who have been to London or Canada.

Can you think of more ways to find information?

1 Read the instructions.    **3** Collect information. 

2 Talk about them in German.     **4** Make a poster. 

Look it up

A

a/an	ein, eine, einer
a lot of ...	viele
a quarter past ...	viertel nach ...
a quarter to ...	viertel vor ...
about	über
absurd	absurd
act out	vorspielen, aufführen
after	nach
afternoon	der Nachmittag
again	wieder
all	alle, alles
am, (I am)	bin, (ich bin)
and	und
angry	wütend
animal	das Tier
anorak	der Anorak
answer	die Antwort, antworten
apple	der Apfel
are, (you are)	bist/sind, (du bist, ihr seid)
arm	der Arm
as	als
at	an/bei/in/um
autumn	der Herbst

B

back	zurück
bacon	der Speck
banana	die Banane
basket	der Korb
basketball	der Basketball
bat	die Fledermaus
be	sein (wie: lustig *sein*)
beak	der Schnabel
because	weil
behind	hinter
big	groß
bike	das Fahrrad
bird	der Vogel
birthday	der Geburtstag
black	schwarz
blackboard	die (grüne) Tafel
board	die Tafel (in England meist weiß)
board game	das Brettspiel
body	der Körper
body part	das Körperteil
book	das Buch
boots	die Stiefel
bottle	die Flasche
boy	der Junge
bread	das Brot
breakfast	das Frühstück
breeze	die Windböe, die Brise
bridge	die Brücke
British	britisch
brother	der Bruder
budgie	der Wellensittich
build a snowman	einen Schneemann bauen
bus	der Bus
butter	die Butter
buy	kaufen
bye-bye	Tschüss

C

cake	der Kuchen, die Torte
call	(an)rufen
can/can not	können/nicht können
candle	die Kerze
cap	die Kappe

carrot	die Karotte
cat	die Katze
catch	fangen
chair	der Stuhl
chalk	die Kreide
cheese	der Käse
chicken	das Huhn
child, children	das Kind, die Kinder
chocolate bar	der Schokoriegel
church	die Kirche
circle	der Kreis, einkreisen
clap	klatschen
class	die Klasse
classroom	das Klassenzimmer
clock	die Uhr
close	schließen
clothes	die Kleidung
cloud	die Wolke
cloudy	bewölkt
coffee	der Kaffee
coin	die Münze
cold	kalt
collect	sammeln
colour	die Farbe, anmalen
coloured pencil	der Buntstift
come	kommen
compare	vergleichen
complete	vervollständigen
copy	abschreiben
count	zählen
cow	die Kuh
create	entwerfen, erstellen
cucumber	die Salatgurke
cut	schneiden
cycling/ride my bike	Rad fahren

D

day	der Tag
dead	tot
dear	lieb, lieber, liebe
dialogue	der Dialog
diary	der Kalender
dice	der Würfel
different	unterschiedlich
dinner	das warme Essen
do/do not	machen/Mach nicht ...!
dog	der Hund
double-decker bus	der Doppeldeckerbus
draw	zeichnen
dress	das Kleid
dress up	verkleiden
drink	das Getränk, trinken
duck	die Ente

E

ear	das Ohr
eat	essen
egg	das Ei
evening	der Abend
everybody	jeder, jede
explain	erklären

F

false	falsch
family	die Familie
Fancy that	Na so was!
father	der Vater
favourite	lieblings-
feather	die Feder
feed	füttern
feet	die Füße

ferris wheel	das Riesenrad
fill	füllen
find	finden
find out	herausfinden
fine	gut
finger	der Finger
finish	das Ziel
firework	das Feuerwerk
fish and chips	Fisch und Pommes Frites
flash	der Blitz
fly	die Fliege, fliegen
fly a kite	einen Drachen steigen lassen
foggy	neblig
food	das Essen
foot	der Fuß
football	der Fußball
forget	vergessen
fresh	frisch
friend	der Freund, die Freundin
from	von
fruit	das Obst
fur	das Fell

G

game	das Spiel
get up	aufstehen
girl	das Mädchen
give	geben
gloves	die Handschuhe
glue stick	der Klebestift
go	gehen
goat	die Ziege
good	gut

grandfather	der Großvater
grandmother	die Großmutter
Great Britain	Großbritannien
great	toll, super
group	die Gruppe
guess	raten
guinea pig	das Meerschweinchen

H

half past (nine)	halb (zehn)
hamster	der Hamster
hand out	austeilen
hand	die Hand
happy	glücklich, froh
has/has not	hat/hat nicht
have a picnic	ein Picknick machen
have/have not	haben/nicht haben
he	er
head	der Kopf
headphones	die Kopfhörer
help	die Hilfe, helfen
her	ihr (wie: *ihr* Buch)
Here you are.	Bitteschön.
here	hier
his	sein (wie: *sein* Buch)
honey	der Honig
horse	das Pferd
hot	heiß
house	das Haus
how	wie
hungry	hungrig
Hurry up!	Beeil dich!

I

I	ich
ice cream	die Eiscreme

idea . . . . die Idee
in . . . . in
in front of . . . . . . vor
is . . . . ist (wie: er *ist*)
it . . . . es
its . . . . sein, ihr (wie: *sein/ihr*
          Fell)

J

jam . . . . die Marmelade
jar (of jam) . . . . . das Marmeladenglas
jeans . . . . die Jeans
juice . . . . der Saft
jump . . . . springen, hüpfen

K

keep . . . . bleiben
keyword . . . . das Schlüsselwort
know . . . . wissen

L

label . . . . beschriften
lady . . . . die Dame
language . . . . . die Sprache
leave . . . . lassen
left . . . . links
leg . . . . das Bein
lesson . . . . die Unterrichtsstunde
let's . . . . Lass/Lasst uns
lift . . . . heben
lightning . . . . . . das Gewitter
like . . . . mögen
line . . . . die Zeile
listen (to) . . . . . zuhören
little . . . . klein
lollipop . . . . der Lutscher
look up . . . . nachschlagen

loud . . . . laut
lunch . . . . das Mittagessen
lunchbox . . . . . die Brotdose
lunchtime . . . . . die Mittagspause

M

many . . . . viel, viele, vieles
map . . . . die Karte
mark . . . . markieren
material . . . . . . das Material
me . . . . mich
meet . . . . treffen
mice . . . . die Mäuse
milk . . . . die Milch, melken
mix . . . . mischen
more . . . . mehr
morning . . . . . . der Morgen
most . . . . meist, höchst
mother . . . . die Mutter
mouse . . . . die Maus
much . . . . viel
muesli . . . . das Müsli
mug . . . . der Becher
my . . . . mein, meine

N

name . . . . der Name, benennen
need . . . . brauchen
new . . . . neu
next . . . . als nächstes, nächste
next to . . . . neben
nice . . . . schön
no . . . . nein
nose . . . . die Nase
not . . . . nicht
now . . . . jetzt

number	die Nummer

O

... o'clock	... Uhr
old	alt
on	auf, im
organise	organisieren
our	unser

P

pack	(ein)packen
paintbox	der Malkasten
paintbrush	der Pinsel
pair	das Paar, paaren
palace	der Palast
pancake	der Pfannkuchen
paper	das Papier
pen	der Füller
pencil	der Bleistift
pencil case	das Mäppchen
pet	das Haustier, streicheln
picture	das Bild
piece	das Stück
pig	das Schwein
piggy bank	das Sparschwein
play	spielen
play croquet	Krocket spielen
play hockey	Hockey spielen
play tennis	Tennis spielen
play the recorder	Blockflöte spielen
please	bitte
poem	das Gedicht
point	zeigen
postcard	die Postkarte
poster	das Poster

practise	üben
present	das Geschenk
presentation	die Präsentation
pullover	der Pullover
punch	der Locher
punnet	das Körbchen, die Schale (für Obst)
put	legen
put on	anziehen

Q

quiet	leise, ruhig, still

R

rabbit	das Kaninchen
rainbow	der Regenbogen
raincoat	der Regenmantel
raindrop	der Regentropfen
rainy	regnerisch
read	lesen
remember	erinnern
repeat	wiederholen
rest	sich ausruhen
rhyme	der Reim
ride a bike	Fahrrad fahren
ride a horse	reiten
right	richtig, rechts
role-play	das Rollenspiel
roll (a dice)	würfeln
rubber	der Radierer
ruler	das Lineal
rumble	das Grollen
run	laufen, rennen

S

sad	traurig

salad	der Salat		spider	die Spinne
salami	die Salami		sponge	der Schwamm
sausage	das Würstchen		spring	der Frühling
say	sagen		stamp	stampfen
scarf	der Schal		stand	stehen
school	die Schule		start	beginnen
school bag	der Schulranzen		sticker	der Aufkleber
school things	die Schulsachen		stormy	stürmisch
season	die Jahreszeit		story	die Geschichte
see	sehen		straight ahead	geradeaus
sentence	der Satz		sugar	der Zucker
share	teilen		summer	der Sommer
sharpener	der Spitzer		sunny	sonnig
she	sie (wie: *sie* geht)		swallow	(ver)schlucken
sheep	das Schaf, die Schafe		sweets	die Süßigkeiten
shirt	das Hemd		swim	schwimmen
shoes	die Schuhe			

T

shop	der Laden, einkaufen		table	der Tisch
shopping centre	das Einkaufszentrum		tail	der Schwanz
shorts	die Shorts		take	nehmen
shout	rufen		take off	ausziehen
sight	die Sehenswürdigkeit		take photos	Fotos machen
sing	singen		talk	sprechen
sister	die Schwester		task	die Aufgabe
sit	sitzen		taxi	das Taxi
ski	Ski, Ski fahren		tea	der Tee
skirt	der Rock		teacher	der Lehrer, die Lehrerin
small	klein		telephone	das Telefon
snowboard	das Snowboard, Snowboard fahren		tell	erzählen, sagen
snowy	schneiend, verschneit		text	der Text
sock	die Socke		thank you/thanks	danke
Sorry, …	Tut mir leid.		the	der, die, das
sound	der Klang		there	da
speak	sprechen		they	sie (wie: *sie* sind da)
spell	buchstabieren			

thing	das Ding, die Sache
think	denken, glauben
this	dies
throw	werfen
thunder	der Donner
tick	ankreuzen (mit Häkchen)
tiggle (tickle)	kitzeln (nur poetisch)
time	die Zeit
tip	der Tipp
tired	müde
to	bis, nach, zu
toast	der Toast
toe	die Fußzehe
together	zusammen
tomato	die Tomate
too	zu, auch (wie: *zu* viel oder du *auch*?)
touch	berühren, anfassen
tractor	der Traktor
trainers	die Turnschuhe
trousers	die Hosen
true	richtig, wahr
try	versuchen
T-shirt	das T-Shirt
turn around	(sich) umdrehen

U

under	unter
underground	die U-Bahn (in London)
us	uns

V

very	sehr

W

walk	laufen, gehen
walk the dog	mit dem Hund Gassi gehen
want	wollen
warm	warm
watch	anschauen
watch TV	fernsehen
water	das Wasser
we	wir
weather	das Wetter
weather forecast	die Wettervorhersage
weekend	das Wochenende
Well done.	Gut gemacht.
what	was
when	wann
where	wo
who	wer
wiggle	wackeln
windy	windig
wing	der Flügel
winter	der Winter
with	mit
woolly hat	die Mütze (aus Wolle)
word	das Wort
work	arbeiten
wriggle	herumzappeln
write (down)	(auf)schreiben
wrong	falsch

Y

year	das Jahr
yes	ja
you	du
your	dein, deine